CUSTOMER OBSESSION

Transform your business with exceptional customer service.

TABLE OF CONTENT

INTRODUCTION

In today's fast-paced business world, the customer is king. To thrive and succeed, companies must go above and beyond to satisfy their customer's needs and provide exceptional service. This is where customer obsession comes in.

Customer obsession is not simply about meeting customer expectations but about exceeding them. It is about building long-term relationships with customers and creating experiences that leave them feeling valued and appreciated. It is about making the customer the focus of every decision, every process, and every action.

In this book, we will explore the importance of customer obsession and how it can transform your business. We will delve into the strategies, and best practices companies can employ to become genuinely customer-centric, from understanding your customers to anticipating their needs and delivering personalized service.

We will also examine case studies of companies that have successfully implemented customer obsession and its positive impact on their business. From startups to Fortune 500 companies, we will see how customer obsession has enabled these organizations to build strong customer relationships, increase loyalty, and drive growth and profitability.

But customer obsession is not just a strategy or a buzzword; it is a mindset. It requires a fundamental shift in organizational culture and a commitment to continuous improvement. This book will provide practical advice on how to foster a culture of customer obsession within your organization and empower your team to provide exceptional service.

Whether you are a small business owner, a manager, or an entrepreneur, Customer Obsession is a must-read for anyone who wants to stay ahead of the competition and create a truly customer-centric organization. So join us on this journey as we explore the power of customer obsession and how it can transform your business.

CHAPTER 1

Understanding Your Customers

As a business owner or marketer, your success depends on your ability to understand your customers. Understanding your customers' needs, preferences, and pain points is crucial for creating products and services that meet their expectations and developing marketing campaigns that resonate with them. In this chapter, we'll explore the importance of understanding your customers and the key factors that influence their behavior.

The Basics of Customer Understanding

At its core, customer understanding is about knowing who your customers are, what they need, and what motivates them to make a purchase. It's about creating a clear picture of your ideal customer and tailoring your products, services, and marketing efforts to meet their unique needs and preferences. But how do you go about understanding your customers?

The first step is to conduct thorough research. This may include market research, customer surveys, focus groups, and social media listening. By gathering data on your customers, you can gain insights into their behavior, preferences, and pain points. This information can then be used to develop a customer persona, which is a detailed profile of your ideal customer.

A customer persona should include demographic information such as age, gender, income, education, and location. It should also include psychographic information such as values, interests, hobbies, and personality traits. By creating a detailed customer persona, you can better understand your customers and develop products, services, and marketing campaigns that resonate with them.

Factors That Influence Customer Behavior

Understanding your customers also requires an understanding of the factors that influence their behavior. These may include internal factors such as motivation, personality, and attitudes, as well as external factors such as culture, social class, and reference groups.

Motivation is a crucial internal factor that drives customer behavior. Customers may be motivated by a desire for status, self-esteem, security, or self-actualization. By understanding what motivates your customers, you can develop products and services that meet their needs and address their desires.

Personality is another internal factor that can influence customer behavior. Personality traits such as extraversion, openness, conscientiousness, agreeableness, and neuroticism can impact how customers perceive and respond to marketing messages. By tailoring your marketing efforts to different personality types, you can increase the effectiveness of your campaigns.

Culture is a significant external factor that can impact customer behavior. Cultural values, beliefs, and norms can influence how customers perceive and respond to products and services. For example, in some cultures, modesty and humility are highly valued, while in others, wealth and status are more important. By understanding cultural differences, you can tailor your products and marketing efforts to be more effective in different regions and markets.

Social class is another external factor that can impact customer behavior. Customers from different social classes may have different needs, preferences, and purchasing habits. By understanding the social class of your customers, you can develop products and marketing campaigns that resonate with their unique needs and desires.

Reference groups are also critical external factors that can influence customer behavior. These may include family, friends, coworkers, and online communities. By understanding the reference groups that your customers belong to, you can develop marketing campaigns that leverage their influence and create social proof for your products and services.

Now that we have a basic understanding of who our customers are, it's time to dig deeper and gather more information about their needs, preferences, and behaviors. One of the most effective ways to do this is by conducting market research.

Market research is the process of gathering and analyzing information about a specific market, including its size, trends, and customer preferences. There are two main types of market research: primary research and secondary research.

Primary research involves collecting new data directly from customers through methods such as surveys, focus groups, and interviews. This type of research can provide valuable insights into customer behavior and preferences, but it can also be time-consuming and expensive.

Secondary research, on the other hand, involves analyzing existing data that has already been collected by others, such as government agencies, industry associations, and market research firms. This data can include demographic information, market size and trends, and competitor analysis.

Both primary and secondary research have their advantages and disadvantages, and the choice between them will depend on a variety of factors, including a budget, time constraints, and the specific information needed.

Another essential tool for understanding your customers is **data analytics.**

In today's digital age, businesses have access to vast amounts of data about their customers, from website traffic and social media engagement to sales and customer service interactions.

Data analytics involves using statistical methods and software to analyze this data and identify patterns and insights that can inform business decisions. For example, data analytics can help businesses identify which products or services are most popular among their customers, which marketing channels are driving the most traffic and conversions, and which customer segments are most profitable.

However, data analytics can also be overwhelming and complex, requiring specialized skills and expertise. Many businesses choose to outsource this function to third-party analytics firms or hire dedicated data analysts.

In addition to market research and data analytics, there are other ways to gather insights into your customers' needs and preferences. One practical approach is to talk to your customers and listen to their feedback simply.

This can be done through customer service interactions, social media engagement, and other channels. By actively seeking out and responding to customer feedback, businesses can demonstrate their commitment to customer satisfaction and gain valuable insights into areas where they can improve.

Another critical aspect of understanding your customers is **developing buyer personas.**

Creating buyer personas is a crucial step in understanding your customers and tailoring your marketing efforts to meet their specific needs. Buyer personas are fictional, generalized representations of your ideal customers. These personas are based on research and data about your existing customers, as well as insights you gather from other sources, such as market research and customer feedback.

By creating buyer personas, businesses can gain a deeper understanding of their customer's needs, motivations, and pain points. This allows companies to tailor their marketing efforts to be more effective and efficient. For example, if your business sells high-end fitness equipment, you might create a buyer persona for a busy professional in their 30s who values health and fitness but has limited time to work out. This persona would inform the messaging, channels, and tactics you use to reach this target customer, such as targeting social media ads to people in this age range who live in metropolitan areas.

Furthermore, buyer personas can help businesses identify gaps in their products or services that may be hindering customer satisfaction or retention. By understanding what your customers truly need and want, you can adjust your offerings to meet their needs better and build stronger relationships with them.

Overall, creating buyer personas can be a potent tool for businesses looking to understand their customers better and tailor their marketing efforts to be more effective. By investing time and resources into creating accurate and detailed buyer personas, businesses can gain a competitive edge in today's crowded marketplace.

ACTION EXERCISES

Conduct customer surveys: One of the best ways to understand your customers is by asking them directly. Design a survey with questions about their demographics, preferences, and behaviors. Use this information to create a detailed customer profile that will help you tailor your marketing and product development efforts to their needs.

Analyze website and social media analytics: Use a website and social media analytics to gain insights into your customers' online behaviors. Look for patterns in their browsing and purchasing habits, and identify the types of content they engage with the most. This data can help you create more effective marketing campaigns and refine your customer personas.

Conduct interviews with customers: Set up interviews with a selection of your most valuable customers to gain deeper insights into their needs, motivations, and pain points. Use this information to create more detailed and accurate buyer personas that will enable you to make more targeted marketing and product development strategies.

Use data analysis tools: Use data analysis tools to segment your customer base and identify key customer groups. Look for commonalities in their behavior, preferences, and demographics, and use this information to create detailed buyer personas that will help you tailor your marketing and product development efforts to their needs.

Monitor customer feedback: Monitor customer feedback on social media, review sites, and customer support channels to gain insights into their experiences with your brand. Use this information to identify pain points and areas for improvement, and use these insights to refine your buyer personas

Chapter 2

Creating a Customer-Centric Culture

In today's business landscape, customer satisfaction is more important than ever before. With increased competition and the rise of social media, a single negative customer experience can have a ripple effect on your company's reputation and bottom line. As a result, more and more businesses are recognizing the importance of creating a customer-centric culture.

But what exactly does a customer-centric culture entail? At its core, it means putting the customer at the center of everything you do. This includes not only delivering a high-quality product or service, but also providing an exceptional customer experience from start to finish.

Creating a customer-centric culture requires a fundamental shift in mindset. It's not just about paying lip service to customer satisfaction, but truly internalizing the belief that the customer comes first. This means understanding your customers' needs, wants, and pain points, and using that knowledge to guide every decision your company makes.

How can you begin to create a customer-centric culture within your organization?

Here are some key steps to get started:

Define your customer experience vision

Before you can create a customer-centric culture, you need to have a clear vision of what that looks like. This means defining your ideal customer experience and setting goals to achieve it. Consider the following questions:

What do you want your customers to feel when they interact with your company?

What kind of experience do you want to provide at every touch point?

How will you measure success in terms of customer satisfaction?

Once you have a clear vision in mind, communicate it to your team and make it a central part of your company culture.

Collect customer feedback

To truly understand your customers' needs and pain points, you need to collect feedback from them on a regular basis. This can be done through surveys, focus groups, or simply by encouraging customers to share their thoughts and experiences with you.

When collecting feedback, be sure to listen carefully to what your customers are saying. Don't just focus on positive feedback – pay attention to any negative feedback as well. Use this feedback to identify areas where you can improve and make changes to better meet your customers' needs.

Empower your employees

Creating a customer-centric culture requires buy-in from your entire team. This means empowering your employees to make decisions and take actions that prioritize the customer experience.

Provide your team with the tools and training they need to deliver exceptional customer service. Encourage them to take ownership of the customer experience and give them the freedom to make decisions that will benefit the customer.

Lead by example

Creating a customer-centric culture starts at the top. As a leader, it's important to set the tone for the entire organization. This means modeling the behavior you want to see in your team and consistently prioritizing the customer experience in all of your decisions.

Be visible and accessible to your team, and encourage open communication and feedback. Show your team that you value their input and are committed to creating a culture that puts the customer first.

Integrate customer-centricity into your processes and systems

In order to truly embed a customer-centric culture within your organization, it's important to integrate customer-centricity into your processes and systems. This means designing processes and systems that prioritize the customer experience at every step of the way.

For example, you may want to redesign your customer service process to be more responsive to customer needs. Or you may want to update your website to make it easier for customers to find the information they need.

Measure and track customer satisfaction

Measuring and tracking customer satisfaction is essential for any business that wants to create a customer-centric culture. This means setting clear metrics for customer satisfaction and tracking them over time.

There are a variety of ways to measure customer satisfaction, including surveys, social media monitoring, and customer reviews. Use these metrics to identify areas where you need to improve and make changes to better meet your customers' needs.

Celebrate successes and learn from failures

Creating a customer-centric culture is an ongoing process. It's important to celebrate successes along the way and use failures as opportunities to learn and grow.

When your team delivers exceptional customer service, take the time to recognize and celebrate their efforts. And when things don't go as planned, use it as an opportunity to identify areas where you need to improve and make changes for the future.

CHAPTER 3

Providing Exceptional Customer Service

Providing exceptional customer service is critical to the success of any business. In today's competitive marketplace, customers have more options than ever before, and they are increasingly likely to switch to a competitor if they have a poor experience with a company. On the other hand, businesses that prioritize the customer experience can build a loyal customer base and differentiate themselves from their competitors.

What Does It Take To Provide Exceptional Customer Service ?

There are a few key elements that can help businesses to deliver a memorable and positive customer experience.

prioritize responsiveness.

Customers expect fast and efficient service, and they won't tolerate long wait times or slow response times. This means having the right systems and processes in place to ensure that customers can quickly and easily get in touch with a representative when they have a question or concern.

One effective way to improve responsiveness is to leverage technology. Many businesses now offer self-service options, such as chatbots or online support forums, which can help customers to quickly find the information they need without having to wait on hold or navigate a complex phone tree. Other businesses may choose to offer 24/7 customer support or prioritize responses to social media inquiries to ensure that customers can get in touch with them at any time.

Personalization.

Customers want to feel valued and appreciated, and they are more likely to remain loyal to a business that takes the time to get to know them and tailor their experience accordingly. This means collecting customer data and using it to deliver personalized recommendations, offers, and content.

One effective way to personalize the customer experience is to use customer relationship management (CRM) software. This type of software allows businesses to store customer data, track interactions, and identify opportunities for upselling or cross-selling. Businesses can also use this data to segment their customers and deliver targeted marketing campaigns that are more likely to resonate with individual customers.

Empathy.

Customers want to feel heard and understood, and they appreciate businesses that take the time to listen to their concerns and offer thoughtful solutions. This means training employees to actively listen to customers, ask probing questions, and demonstrate empathy and understanding.

One effective way to improve empathy is to use active listening techniques. This involves giving the customer your full attention, repeating back what they've said to confirm your understanding, and asking follow-up questions to ensure that you fully understand their needs and concerns. It's also important to remain calm and patient, even in challenging situations, and to focus on finding a solution that works for the customer.

Focusing on continuous improvement.

This means regularly soliciting feedback from customers, analyzing customer data to identify areas for improvement, and implementing changes to address customer pain points.

One effective way to improve continuous improvement is to use a feedback loop. This involves regularly surveying customers to gather feedback on their experience, analyzing the data to identify trends and areas for improvement, and then implementing changes to address these issues. By continuously refining the customer experience, businesses can stay ahead of their competitors and ensure that they are delivering the best possible service to their customers.

Going above and beyond to exceed customer expectations

Going above and beyond to exceed customer expectations is all about providing exceptional service that goes beyond the norm. It's about doing everything in your power to make your customers feel special, appreciated, and taken care of. When you go above and beyond, you create a lasting impression that not only meets their needs but also exceeds them.

So, how can you provide exceptional service that exceeds customer expectations?

Anticipate their needs before they even ask.

Think ahead and take proactive steps to provide what they might need or want. For instance, if you're a server at a restaurant and a customer spills their drink, you can bring them a fresh napkin before they even ask.

Personalize the experience for your customers.

Use their name, preferences, and past interactions to tailor your service to their individual needs. This makes them feel valued and appreciated. For example, if you work at a hotel, you can offer a customer their favorite type of pillow or remember their favorite dish and recommend it when they come to the restaurant.

When a customer has a problem or complaint, take ownership of the issue, apologize for any inconvenience caused, and work with them to find a solution that meets their needs. This shows that you care about their satisfaction and are committed to resolving the issue as quickly and effectively as possible.

Providing unexpected perks or benefits

This is another way to exceed customer expectations. Offer a free upgrade, provide a personalized note or gift, or give them a discount or coupon for their next purchase. These little extras can make a big impact and set you apart from your competitors.

CHAPTER 4

Leveraging Technology for Customer Success

It has become increasingly essential in recent times for businesses to leverage technology to enhance customer success. In today's world, customers expect a seamless experience when interacting with a company, whether it's through a website, mobile app, or in-person interaction. To meet these expectations and stay competitive, companies must adopt new technologies and strategies that prioritize customer success.

Key Technologies That Businesses Can Leverage For Customer Success

Customer relationship management (CRM) software.

CRM software enables companies to centralize customer data, automate customer interactions, and personalize the customer experience. With a CRM system, businesses can better understand their customers' needs and preferences, anticipate them, and proactively address any issues that may arise.

Artificial intelligence (AI).

Artificial intelligence (AI) is revolutionizing how businesses interact with customers. AI-powered tools and chatbots can be used to provide personalized customer support, answer common customer questions, and even anticipate customer needs before they arise.

Businesses can use AI for customer success by providing personalized product recommendations. By analyzing customer data such as purchase history, browsing behavior, and demographic information, AI algorithms can generate tailored recommendations that are highly relevant to the customer's preferences and needs. This not only improves the customer's experience by providing them with products they are more likely to purchase but also increases the likelihood of repeat business and customer loyalty.

AI-powered chatbots are another powerful tool for improving customer success. By integrating chatbots into their websites or social media platforms, businesses can provide 24/7 customer support without the need for human operators. Chatbots can answer common customer questions, such as product availability, pricing, and shipping information, and can even handle basic transactions, such as order cancellations or returns. By reducing wait times and providing instant support, chatbots can significantly improve the customer experience and increase customer satisfaction.

In addition to providing reactive support, AI can also be used to anticipate customer needs and proactively offer solutions. For example, by analyzing customer data, AI algorithms can identify patterns and trends that indicate when a customer is likely to need additional support or when they may be considering a new purchase. Businesses can then use this information to reach out to the customer with personalized offers or recommendations, effectively providing a level of support that the customer may not have even realized they needed.

Another way businesses can leverage AI for customer success is by using predictive analytics to identify and address potential issues before they become significant problems. By analyzing customer data and monitoring for anomalies or patterns that indicate a potential issue, businesses can proactively reach out to the customer to resolve the issue before it becomes a significant source of frustration. This not only improves the customer experience but also reduces the workload on customer support teams, who can focus on more complex issues that require human intervention.

SOCIAL MEDIA

In addition to CRM and AI, businesses can leverage social media to enhance customer success.

Social media has become an increasingly powerful business tool to enhance customer success. With millions of people using social media platforms daily, companies can leverage these platforms to reach a large audience and build relationships with customers in real-time.

One of the key benefits of using social media for customer success is the ability to engage with customers in real time. By monitoring social media channels and responding promptly to customer inquiries and concerns, businesses can demonstrate their commitment to customer satisfaction and build trust with their audience. This not only helps to resolve customer issues quickly but also creates a positive impression of the business and can lead to increased customer loyalty.

Another way businesses can use social media to enhance customer success is by sharing content that resonates with their audience. By creating and sharing valuable content, such as blog posts, infographics, and videos, businesses can educate and inform their customers, demonstrate their expertise in their field, and provide added value to their audience. This can help to establish the company as a thought leader in their industry and further strengthen the relationship with their customers.

Furthermore, social media can be used to foster brand loyalty by providing customers with exclusive offers, promotions, and discounts. By rewarding customers for their dedication, businesses can increase customer retention, attract new customers through referrals, and ultimately drive revenue growth.

It's vital for businesses to approach social media with a strategic mindset and integrate it into their overall customer success strategy. This means identifying the social media platforms that are most relevant to their target audience, developing a content strategy that aligns with their brand messaging and measuring the success of their social media efforts through metrics such as engagement rates, follower growth, and customer satisfaction scores.

Overall, social media presents a valuable opportunity for businesses to enhance customer success and build lasting relationships with their customers. By engaging with customers in real time, sharing helpful content, and fostering brand loyalty, businesses can differentiate themselves from their competitors and achieve long-term success.

However, it's important to note that simply adopting new technologies alone is insufficient to ensure customer success. Businesses must also develop and implement a comprehensive customer success strategy that encompasses people, processes, and technology. This means identifying key customer touch points, developing metrics to measure success, and aligning internal teams around a shared customer success vision.

Moreover, it's crucial to prioritize customer privacy and data security when leveraging technology for customer success. Businesses must ensure that customer data is collected and stored securely and that customer privacy is always protected. This requires investing in robust security measures, such as encryption and multi-factor authentication, and developing policies and procedures that govern data access and usage.

CHAPTER 5

Measuring and Improving Customer Satisfaction

Customer satisfaction has become increasingly crucial in today's fiercely competitive business environment. As consumers have access to a plethora of options, businesses that prioritize customer satisfaction stand a better chance of retaining their current customer base, drawing in new customers, and attaining long-term success.

But how do businesses measure and improve customer satisfaction? In this chapter, we will explore the importance of measuring customer satisfaction, the methods and tools used to measure it, and strategies for improving it.

Why Measuring Customer Satisfaction Matters:

Measuring customer satisfaction is important for several reasons. First, it helps businesses understand how their customers perceive their products, services, and brand. By identifying areas where customers are satisfied and areas where they are dissatisfied, businesses can make informed decisions about where to focus their efforts to improve the customer experience.

Second, measuring customer satisfaction can help businesses identify trends and patterns in customer behavior. For example, if customers consistently report issues with a particular product feature or customer service process, businesses can address these issues to improve customer satisfaction and loyalty.

Finally, measuring customer satisfaction can help businesses track their progress over time. By regularly measuring customer satisfaction and comparing results over time, businesses can identify areas where they have made progress and areas where they still need to improve.

Methods for Measuring Customer Satisfaction:

There are several methods that businesses can use to measure customer satisfaction. Some of the most common methods include customer surveys, customer feedback forms, online reviews, and social media monitoring.

CUSTOMER SURVEYS

Customer surveys are one of the most effective ways to measure customer satisfaction. Surveys can be conducted online, through email, or in-person, and can be designed to gather feedback on specific products, services, or interactions with the business. The key to a successful survey is to ask the right questions and use a reliable and valid survey instrument.

CUSTOMER FEEDBACK FORMS

Customer feedback forms can be used to collect feedback from customers at various touch points throughout the customer journey. For example, businesses can ask customers to provide feedback after making a purchase, after receiving customer support, or after visiting a physical location. Feedback forms can be paper-based or digital, and can be designed to gather both quantitative and qualitative feedback.

ONLINE REVIEWS

Online reviews are another important source of customer feedback. Customers can leave reviews on third-party review sites such as Yelp or Google, or on the business's own website. Businesses can use online reviews to identify areas where they are doing well and areas where they need to improve.

SOCIAL MEDIA MONITORING

Social media monitoring involves tracking and analyzing customer conversations on social media platforms such as Twitter, Facebook, and Instagram. By monitoring social media conversations, businesses can identify customer complaints, respond to customer inquiries and feedback, and gather insights into customer preferences and behavior.

Strategies for Improving Customer Satisfaction:

Once businesses have identified areas where customer satisfaction can be improved, they can develop and implement strategies to address these areas. Some strategies for improving customer satisfaction include:

Improving product or service quality: If customers are dissatisfied with a particular product or service, businesses can focus on improving the quality of that product or service.

Enhancing customer support: Businesses can provide training to customer support teams to ensure that they are able to provide effective and timely support to customers.

Personalizing the customer experience: By collecting customer data and using it to personalize the customer experience, businesses can improve customer satisfaction and loyalty.

Communicating with customers: Businesses can proactively communicate with customers to keep them informed about new products, services, or updates.

Offering incentives: Businesses can offer incentives such as discounts or loyalty rewards to customers who provide feedback or refer new customers.

CHAPTER 6

Fixing Customer Indecision

Customer indecision can be frustrating for businesses, primarily when they have invested time and effort into attracting potential customers. However, understanding why customers hesitate to purchase can help enterprises overcome this challenge and increase their conversion rates.

Reasons for Customer Indecision:

There can be several reasons why customers hesitate to make a purchase. Some of the common ones are:

Lack of information: Customers may be indecisive because they need more information about the product or service they are interested in. They may question its features, benefits, pricing, or how it compares to similar products or services.

Fear of making the wrong decision: Customers may fear making the bad decision and regretting their purchase later. They may want to research more or seek opinions from others before making a decision.

Financial constraints: Customers may hesitate to purchase due to economic conditions. They may need clarification on whether they can afford the product or service or if it provides enough value for the price.

Indecisive personality traits: Some customers may have a natural tendency towards indecision, making it difficult to make a purchase decision.

Strategies to Overcome Customer Indecision:

Provide clear and detailed information: Businesses can overcome customer indecision by providing precise and detailed information about their products or services. This can include product features, benefits, pricing, and how it compares to similar products or services. Providing comprehensive report can help customers make an informed decision and increase their confidence in the product or service.

Offer personalized recommendations: Offering customized recommendations is a strategy that can help customers make a more informed decision by tailoring product suggestions based on their preferences and past purchase history. Using data analysis and customer behavior tracking, businesses can offer customers personalized recommendations relevant to their interests and needs. Personalized recommendations can be delivered through various channels, including email, social media, or on-site product recommendations.

Provide social proof: Social proof is the concept of leveraging the power of other people's experiences and opinions to influence decision-making. By showcasing customer reviews, ratings, and testimonials, businesses can provide social proof that their products or services are high-quality and worth purchasing. Social proof can be displayed on the company's website, social media channels, and review platforms such as Yelp and Google Reviews.

Create a sense of urgency: Creating a sense of urgency is a strategy that can motivate customers to make a decision quickly by creating the perception that time is running out or the product may not be available soon. your business can achieve this through limited-time offers, discounts, or countdown timers that indicate when the offer will expire. By creating a sense of urgency, businesses can encourage customers to purchase before they miss out on the opportunity.

Offer a guarantee: A satisfaction guarantee is a strategy to help customers feel more confident in their purchase decision. By offering a warranty that assures customers that they can return the product if they are not satisfied, businesses can remove the risk of making a purchase. This can build trust with customers and increase the likelihood of repeat business.

Provide exceptional customer service: Providing excellent customer service is a strategy that can help businesses build trust and loyalty with customers. By providing timely and helpful responses to customer inquiries, resolving issues quickly and effectively, and going above and beyond to meet customer needs, businesses can create a positive customer experience that encourages customers to make a purchase. Exceptional customer service can also result in positive word-of-mouth marketing, further attracting new customers to the business.

CHAPTER 7

Building Loyalty and Advocacy

Building a loyal customer base is essential to your company's success as a business owner. Loyal customers are more likely to buy from you repeatedly, recommend your products or services to others, and leave positive reviews that can help attract new customers. This chapter will discuss the importance of building loyalty and advocacy and some strategies to help you achieve this goal.

The Importance of Loyalty and Advocacy

Loyal customers are the lifeblood of any business. They are more likely to forgive occasional mistakes and overlook minor flaws in your products or services, as they have a solid emotional attachment to your brand. They are also more likely to spend more money on your products or services over time, as they trust your brand and believe in its value.

Advocacy, on the other hand, is when your customers become your brand ambassadors. They actively promote your products or services to their friends, family, and strangers on social media or review sites. This is a powerful marketing tool, as people are likelier to trust recommendations from people they know and respect rather than advertisements or other marketing forms.

Building Loyalty and Advocacy

So, how can you build loyalty and advocacy among your customers? There are several strategies you can use, including:

Personalization: People love feeling like they are being treated as individuals, not just as faceless customers. Personalizing your interactions with your customers can build a stronger emotional connection with them. This could include using their name in emails, offering personalized recommendations based on their previous purchases, or sending them special offers on their birthday or anniversary.

Excellent Customer Service: Your customers expect high-quality customer service, and delivering on this expectation is essential to building loyalty. Ensure your customer service team is knowledgeable, friendly, and responsive to customer needs. Go above and beyond to resolve any issues or concerns your customers may have, and ensure they leave every interaction feeling satisfied.

Reward Programs: Reward programs are a great way to incentivize repeat purchases and build loyalty. Offer your customers points or discounts for every purchase, and allow them to redeem these rewards for complimentary products or services. This will encourage them to keep returning to your business and make them feel appreciated for their loyalty.

Community Building: People love feeling part of a community, and building a sense of community around your brand can help you build loyalty and advocacy. This could include hosting events or webinars, creating a social media group or forum where customers can connect, or even featuring user-generated content on your website or social media accounts.

Asking for Feedback: Don't hesitate to ask your customers for feedback. By asking for their opinions and considering their feedback, you can show your customers that you value their input and care about their experience with your brand. This can help build trust and loyalty over time and can even lead to valuable insights that can help you improve your products or services.

The story of Sophie, the owner of a small online clothing store, illustrates the importance of building loyalty and advocacy among your customers. By personalizing her interactions, offering excellent customer service, implementing reward programs, making sense of community, and asking for feedback, Sophie created a solid emotional connection with her customers and turned them into brand ambassadors. Her loyal customers became the foundation of her business for years to come, helping her grow her customer base and increase her revenue over time. Sophie's story is just one example of how anyone can apply these strategies to any business and how they can lead to long-term success.

Sophie was the owner of a small online clothing store. A handful of loyal customers loved her unique designs and high-quality materials. Still, she knew she needed to do more to build loyalty and advocacy among her customer base.

Sophie decided to start by personalizing her interactions with her customers. She began using their names in her emails and even sent them personalized recommendations based on their previous purchases. Her customers were thrilled to receive these customized messages; many even shared them on social media, spreading the word about Sophie's excellent customer service.

Next, Sophie focused on delivering excellent customer service. She trained her team to be knowledgeable, friendly, and responsive to customer needs. Whenever a customer had an issue or concern, Sophie went above and beyond to resolve it quickly and to the customer's satisfaction.

To incentivize repeat purchases, Sophie created a reward program. She offered her customers points for every purchase they made, which they could redeem for complimentary products or services. Her customers loved this program, and many started making frequent purchases to earn more rewards.

Sophie also wanted to build a sense of community around her brand. She hosted a few virtual events, including webinars on fashion trends and styling tips. She also created a private Facebook group where customers could connect and share their favorite outfits and styling tips. This community quickly became a hub of activity, with customers posting photos and tagging Sophie's brand in their social media posts.

Finally, Sophie asked her customers for feedback on her products and services. She sent out surveys and encouraged her customers to share their opinions. She was pleased to receive lots of constructive feedback, and she used this feedback to improve her designs and website.

As a result of these efforts, Sophie's customer base snowballed. Her loyal customers became her brand ambassadors, leaving positive reviews and recommending her store to friends and family. Sophie's business was thriving, and she knew that it was all thanks to the loyalty and advocacy of her customers. She focused on building these relationships, learning they were the key to her success.

CONCLUSION

As we end this book, I want to speak directly to you, the reader. Throughout these pages, we've explored the importance of practicing customer obsession to achieve long-term success for your business. But what does that mean for you as an individual?

It means that you have the power to make a difference in your organization. You can listen to your customers, understand their needs and preferences, and use that knowledge to create products and services that truly delight them. You can create a customer-centric culture that values the needs and desires of your customers above all else and build strong relationships with them that lead to long-term loyalty and advocacy.

But it's not enough to read this book and nod your head in agreement. It would be best if you took action. You must commit to continuously improving and adapting to changing customer needs and preferences. You must be willing to take bold risks and experiment with new ideas to truly differentiate yourself in the marketplace.

So I challenge you to embrace customer obsession and put it into practice in your work. Please make a commitment to your customers, and work tirelessly to create products and services that truly delight them. The rewards will be immense for your customers and your business.

Thank you for taking the time to read this book and for your commitment to implementing customer obsession. Together, we can create a world where customers are indeed at the center of everything we do.

REMEMBER THIS!

Please leave a review on any of the platforms you purchased this book and tell me how it has helped you

www.ingramcontent.com/pod-product-compliance
Lightning Source LLC
Chambersburg PA
CBHW071143220526
45467CB00015B/1825

* 9 7 9 8 3 8 5 6 1 9 8 7 0 *